GEORGE MICHÆL FACTFILE

George Michæl and Tony Parsons

FANTAIL

Acknowledgements

The authors and publisher would like to thank the following for their help in supplying the photographs reproduced in this book:

Pages 6-7 private source; page 10 Chris Craymer/Scope; page 11 CBS Records; page 12 Brian Aris; page 13 Chris Craymer/Scope; page 14 CBS Records; page 15 Chris Craymer/Scope; page 16 private source; page 17 Chris Craymer/Scope; pages 18-19 Daily Mirror; pages 21-23 Chris Craymer/Scope; pages 25-28 Michael Putland/Retna; page 29 Neil Preston/Camera Five; page 30 Michael Putland/Retna; pages 31-33 Neil Preston/Retna; page 37 London Features International; page 43 Martyn Goddard; page 46 Ollerenshaw/LFI; pages 47-49 Michael Putland/Retna; page 52 Tony McGee; page 54 Martyn Goddard; page 55 Martyn Goddard, Tony McGee; pages 56-57 Martyn Goddard; pages 60-61 Chris Cuffaro/Visages; page 63 Michael Putland/Retna; page 64 Chris Cuffaro; page 66 Chris Cuffaro/Visages; page 68 Chris Cuffaro/Visages; page 70 Michael Putland/Retna; page 71 Chris Cuffaro/Visages; page 73 Chris Cuffaro/Visages; page 74 Michael Putland/Retna; page 79 Chris Cuffaro; pages 80-81 Martyn Goddard; page 83 Michael Putland; pages 91-96 supplied by George Michael.

Thanks also to those photographers not credited, whose names were unavailable at the time of going to press.

FANTAIL BOOKS
Published by the Penguin Group
Penguin Books Ltd, 27 Wrights Lane, London W8 5TZ, England
Penguin Books USA Inc., 375 Hudson Street, New York, New York 10014, USA
Penguin Books Australia Ltd, Ringwood, Victoria, Australia
Penguin Books Canada Ltd, 10 Alcorn Avenue, Toronto, Ontario, Canada M4V 3B2
Penguin Books (NZ) Ltd, 182–190 Wairau Road, Auckland 10, New Zealand

Penguin Books Ltd, Registered Offices: Harmondsworth, Middlesex, England

The unabridged version of the text first published by Michael Joseph 1990
Published in paperback by Penguin Books 1991
This edition, containing new and revised material, published 1992
10 9 8 7 6 5 4 3 2 1

Made and printed in Great Britain by William Clowes Limited, Beccles and London

□ *George:* My name is Georgios Kyriacos Panayiotou. To the outside world I am and always will be known as something else, but it's not my name. □

□ *George:* My parents were rock and roll dancers. They met at a dance and my father used to throw my mother all over the show. There are some really cool pictures of my dad which they never used to show me when I was growing up because they were afraid that I could point to them and say – well, look, *you* did it.

When he was very young my dad was very handsome. My mum sent his picture to a magazine. There used to be a newspaper called *Reveille*, and they used to do a competition called 'Search For A TV Star'. Everybody sent their picture in with a little résumé and my dad got to the final. He got his picture in the paper and he was in the final with one other guy. Mum kept the picture. It said underneath, 'JACK PANOS' – he had shortened the family name to Panos – 'JACK PANOS IS CHASED DOWN THE STREET BY GIRLS WHEREVER HE GOES'. □

Jack the Lad. This picture stayed hidden in the family vault until I was about eighteen - bad example, etc.

Lesley Angold Harrison (the Angold was an inversion of the French family name) defied the ancient barriers of class and country to marry her jiving Greek boyfriend. As Richard Ellman said of Oscar Wilde's mother, 'She was more emancipated than her age'.

Jack remained as close to the huge Panayiotou brood as ever, sending money home to Cyprus and eventually bringing across most of his brothers and sisters (one sister emigrated only as far as Greece), all the while working his way up from the kitchen floor of the catering business and raising a family.

Jack and Lesley's first child was a girl, Yioda, followed by another girl, Melanie, two years later. Two years after that they had their third and final child, a boy they called Georgios Kyriacos Panayiotou, born at 73 Church Lane, Finchley, part of London's endless grey sprawl, on 25 June 1963.

The young me, with Dad and my sisters. Regent's Park methinks.

□ *George:* I have never felt any ethnic connection between the Greeks and me other than how hairy I am. Hirsute. That's a good word. But although I don't feel any real affinity with Greece I'm glad that my father is Mediterranean and I'm not just of English stock. I think I would be a different person, I think I would have grown up with less belief, more reservations about what I wanted to do with my life. I think one of the things that's inherent in British people is that they think they are doing something out of the ordinary if they aspire to be something more than they are. Any kind of social or upward mobility is regarded with suspicion. Well, it was never questioned in my home. I saw it around me all the time. And today when I see people who don't have the nerve to realize their potential, who are too afraid to try, it frustrates the hell out of me. I see it constantly and I think it is a very English thing.

As for my dad, I didn't learn about hard work from him because I could never work as hard as he did. In a sense, what he's done is more of an achievement than what I have – and thousands of people do it – just the idea of coming to a foreign country, working until your fingers bleed to send for your family, to bring them to a country that you arrived in with twenty shillings. □

□ *George:* For the entire year I went to Kingsbury High School, we lived above my dad's restaurant. So I had steak and chips every night, popped down to the restaurant for ice-cream whenever I felt like it – which was often – and in the course of a year I went from being a skinny eleven-year-old to a fat twelve-year-old. It happened at exactly the same time as puberty. From then on I was quite a tubby kid. I never had a gut – I was just kind of *big* all over. I suppose that was why I was never picked on at school. I was never physically weedy – only in my head perhaps. □

□ *Andrew Ridgeley:* It happens all the time at school. You get there in the morning and the teacher says – we've got a new boy, who's going to look after him? They allot the new kid to someone they feel might be responsible. As a junior, I had never been considered responsible enough to have a new kid in my charge – so I was dying to have a go. He was introduced, I put my hand up – and I got him. □

Melanie, Yioda and me.

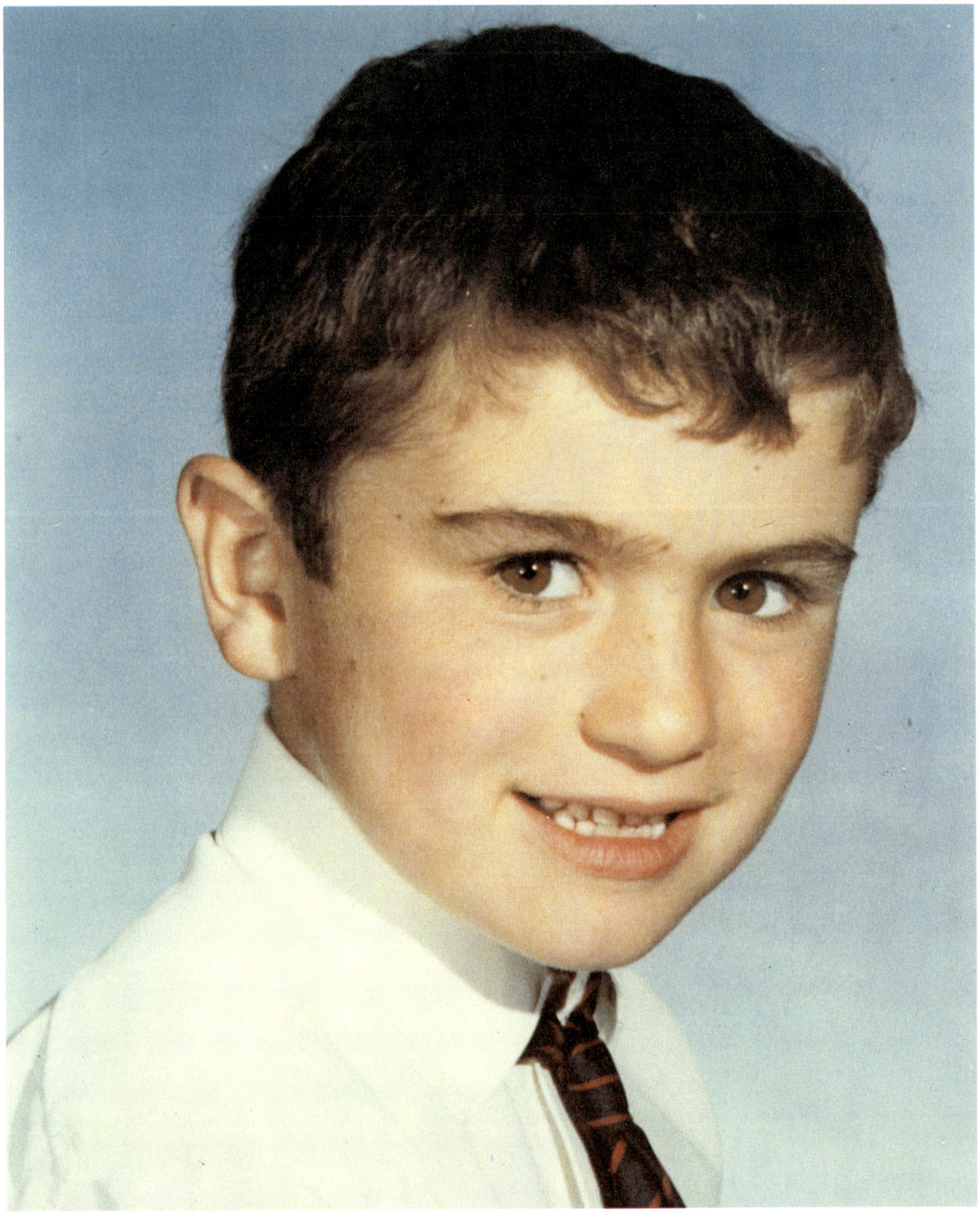

A school photo. (Notice the hair is begining to curl, the cheeks are filling out, soon there won't be a lot to smile about.)

□ *George:* I was a terrible dancer but Andrew and I worked out these routines that we could do at school discos. That would have been when I was fourteen – I had just got my first contact lenses. I put my contacts in and suddenly realized that I wasn't Quasimodo. I actually started getting invited to parties. Before that I was the kid with the sense of humour who would muck about and everybody liked but who didn't get thought about when it came to parties because they didn't expect him to get off with anyone. So I got my contacts. The optician kept saying he's too young, he's too young, but I wanted them so badly… □

Love me, love my donkey. My father's village, Patriki. At the tender age of seven I turned down sponsorship offers from Diet Coke and Bergasol.

George: Anyway, my dad gave up on me when he saw I had no interest in trying to get to university. He was convinced that I was going to be a liability to him when I was thirty, always coming to him for money. Which, in fact, I still do – I don't carry cash around with me.

My parents used to let me bring home anyone I liked – but they didn't like Andrew at all. He was much more confident than they were used to my friends being, he didn't have any of the inhibitions or cautions that most people feel when they walk into someone else's home. He was never like that, he was always himself.

Yog – which is what my closest friends and family call me – comes from Andrew. He was at my house and heard my sisters or mother calling me Georgios – *Yorgos* – which they would shorten to just *Yorg*. And so Andrew went back to school and said, ho-ho-ho, it's really funny round at his house, they all call him *Yog*. Yog – ho-ho – it's like Yoghurt, innit? So I used to get called Yoghurt a lot too.

David Austin and me in my garden, back in the 1960s when it still snowed.

George and Andrew had a vision of the crushing monotony of most adult lives. The pair of them certainly hit a creative streak around this time, working on the songs that would chart their career flight plan for the next few years – 'Wham Rap!', 'Club Tropicana' and 'Careless Whisper'. 'Wham Rap!' would be their début single and the start of the prancing, dancing leather-boy look that would be the distinguishing feature of early Wham! 'Club Tropicana' would steer them away from the street to sunnier, more balmy shores. And 'Careless Whisper' would break hearts and lay the foundation for George Michael's solo career. A classic pop song but charged with real regret, it covered the usual themes of love, temptation and betrayal but with a unique despair, a rare beauty.

□ *George:* We went to music publishers, at Virgin and about a dozen other places, and we used to turn up and pretend we had appointments. Otherwise they would never have agreed to see us...We got into most of the big publishers that way, just turned up and did our routine. They nearly always believed you.

They normally listened to the tape in our presence. Usually they would turn it off after about ten or fifteen seconds. I remember sitting there while they listened to 'Wham Rap!'. We just had this crappy little Doctor Rhythm going boom-cha, boom-cha, boom-cha. They wouldn't even wait for the bass to come in, they would go – tch, another synthesizer band. And we would go, no we just haven't got any money for any drums. The attitude was horrible, really horrible. In a way I can understand it because they see so little talent. □

Mark Dean didn't want anyone to give him a job. Mark Dean wanted someone to give him a record company. CBS, the jolly giant of Soho Square, granted his wish. If they could not get young Dean on their staff then they could still have him on their side, they could still benefit from his magical instincts, his mystical sixth sense, the way he seemed to know *what was going to happen next.* CBS would finance the label, manufacture and distribute its product, and Dean would run it. Profits would be split – even if not down the middle.

Mark Dean's label was called Innervision Records, and the name and the company's logo (a quiffed young man with the word INNERVISION pouring from his eyes like some cosmic hallucination) seemed to revel in his reputation as a hip young soothsayer of teen taste.

A friend eventually persuaded Dean to give the Wham! tape some of his time. He was immediately and wildly enthusiastic. Wham!, born in January, entered negotiations with Innervision in February and were to sign, in a premature ejaculation of agreement (their respective lawyers had not yet completed contractual negotiations), on 24 March.

They were rehearsing at the Halligan Band Centre in Holloway, one of north London's less salubrious outposts, when Dean came in brandishing a contract and insisting that the deal was completed immediately. CBS release schedules were cited as the reason for all the urgency. George, Andrew and Dean walked around the corner to a greasy spoon café and very soon all their signatures were on the contract.

I got the jeans from Woodhouse, the T-shirt and socks from Marks and Spencer (Innervision wardrobe allowance, remember), and the red cheeks from an over-zealous make-up artist.

□ *George:* One of the most incredible moments of my life was hearing 'Careless Whisper' demo'ed properly, with a band and a sax and everything. It was ironic that we signed the contract with Mark that day, the day I finally believed that we had number-one material. The same day we signed it all away. But you can never really know what you are capable of, you can never really have that foresight.

I definitely had the feeling, if I don't sign this, it could all slip away. Everyone tells you that it is only the lucky ones that make it and you think – this is it. This is my lucky break. Later, when people described the contract, they always used the same word – *punitive*. □

An early photographic session. Nice jacket, shame about the carpet.

In April, George and Andrew signed a publishing deal with Morrison–Leahy, a new company set up by Mark Dean's erstwhile mentor, Bryan Morrison, who had once upon a time been the manager of The Pretty Things, and the former owner of GTO Records, Dick Leahy. Tall and thin, tanned and steel-haired, dapper in understated, expensive suits and toting a cigar the size of a small torpedo, Dick Leahy was to become one of the most crucial factors in the career of George Michael, a man who always transcended the traditional role of the publisher.

□ *Dick Leahy:* They walked into the office and almost without hearing the songs you knew that they were going to make it. There was something very, very special about them. They knew exactly what they were going to do. They looked like they were going to do it and I totally believed they were going to do it. There was absolutely no question that these two boys stood out from the crowd – they looked phenomenal. Andrew walked down a street and got a reaction. □

'Wham Rap! (Enjoy What You Do)' was released in June and failed to make an impression on even the lowliest regions of the charts, peaking at an unimpressive hundred and five despite all those night spent hoofing it around those slippery dance floors. This likeable, light-hearted ode to a life beyond the workaday world would have to wait until its rerelease at the end of the winter before winning the affection of the nation.

Early Days With Innervision

At the time of Wham Rap! (Enjoy What You Do)

☐ *Dick Leahy:* 'Wham Rap!' had flopped. That was a great disappointment to George – not so much to me because I always thought he could make a better record of it and in some ways I thought it was a good lesson to learn at that stage. But then 'Young Guns' started going down the charts and that was a dangerous time

George Michael was too good not to have happened but if 'Young Guns' had not happened, I think it would have seriously affected Wham! But fortunately the next week the record went up and then we got *Top of the Pops*. They did *Top of the Pops* on the Thursday when the record was at forty-two and on the Monday morning at CBS distribution centre there were over thirty-thousand orders.

That was the chance to get Wham! across to everyone on just one TV performance. George just didn't go on and do *Top of the Pops*. This was his chance for the big one and he grabbed it. A very well-known manager called me up on the Monday morning and asked me for the name of the choreographer! It was an outstanding live TV performance – and it broke Wham! right open. It took them nationwide. ☐

Wham Rap! ***Miss*** **Young Guns** ***Hit*** **October '82**

Wham! saw out their year of wonders by playing the Christmas concert at their old school, where everyone knew who they were. Workloads and litigation and the shrieking obsession of the gutter Press would soon shade their lives with a darker hue, but for now, with one hit single under their belts, this was a perfect celebration of their success, one that they could share with their hometown friends, one that reflected the strong Mickey Rooney–Judy Garland mondo-show business ethic that ran through the early, pair dancing days of Wham! Hey, they seemed to imply, we can put on the show *right here*.

Dreams can come true, seemed to be the message. It could happen to you.

Remixed and rereleased, the new, improved 'Wham Rap!' climbed into the top ten at number eight in February. It was followed in May by 'Bad Boys', the final part in Wham!'s trilogy of leather-boy street anthems.

It is a sporting truism that champions win even when they are playing badly. 'Bad Boys' was Wham! – and George Michael – with their commercial peak so far and their creative low point in total alignment. This was championship form indeed...and though his solo songwriting effort had not panned out as well as the previous singles, it was already clear that, from here on in, only one man was going to do the writing for the band.

□ *George:* Andrew was really starting to feel my songwriting ambitions begin to accelerate. I wasn't trying to edge him out or anything but it was just so obvious that was where it was going in terms of writing. And it is only because we didn't talk about it that it became a tense subject. But once we talked about it we got it out of the way and we never talked about it again. We never needed to. It wasn't a matter of something we didn't *want* to talk about again. It was always understood how important we were to each other in the framework of the group, and we both understood that the group would have a certain lifespan. The only other thing to be decided was when it would become defunct. And that's what we talked about after the initial confrontation – when would it be time to finish. It was always totally amicable.

But we had one big argument when he felt he was getting nudged out of the writing. Then he said – look, Yog, the easiest and fastest way for us to get to be a really big band is for you to write everything. He may not have wanted it particularly but what he wanted most of all was to be a big star. Everything that we ever wrote together was written before the release of that first single. By the time that 'Bad Boys' came out the friction was increasing – and then he said go ahead and do it.

Some of it was laziness and some of it was that he was losing confidence about his songs in the light of what I was writing. □

Bad Boys. Mean and moody George and Andy, who were, it has to be said, starting to believe in their own Press.
'What was that you said, Andy?'
'I said, suck those cheeks in, you fat bastard.'

□ *Andrew:* Litigation is the abyss. You see it yawning before you and you think – oh God, oh God, I have read about this. It is a time of massive lawyers' bills, a frustrating, anxious time, and George and I were ratty with each other at that point. □

□ *Simon Napier-Bell:* The fight with Innervision was absolutely dirty. I went to every possible means to make sure we won. I provoked Mark Dean into doing something that I felt was a possibility he might do. I had a phone conversation in which I was rude to him and then he wrote me a threatening letter. A threatening letter in abysmal handwriting. It was delivered to my front door by bike and I put it in a safe and when we went to court there it was ready to pull out and show what sort of person Mark Dean was. It's a tough game...

I had to get George and Andrew out of that contract. I am not going to do anything genuinely hurtful or harmful to anybody but I will do anything I can which is legal to win this case for my clients. It was a great battle. Nice to do it, nice to win it... □

□ *George:* It's very tough. Purely for pragmatic business reasons, CBS sided with Wham! instead of Innervision. I'm not comfortable with it but I can be distant from it. It's very easy not to be affected by something like that when you know that you're not going to be the underdog. A business that generally treats artists disgustingly seems to have been quite reasonable to me – probably because I always had what they wanted.

In all its history, CBS has never lost a band. Not through a subsidiary or any other way. We would have been a precedent. And when it looked as it if was going to happen, they stepped in. □

The Great Escape. Just before the legal battle began, we came clean and headed for the beach. Rich and famous here we come . Hello Smash Hits, goodbye NME.

Simon Napier-Bell

EARLY DAYS WITH INNERVISION

CONTRACT FIGHT ENDS *MARCH '84*

☐ *George:* I think 'Go Go' is undoubtedly the most remembered Wham! song – because it is that much more STUPID than anything else! I still look at that video and think it worked perfectly for that song. Really poppy, really colourful – it totally captures that whole period. But although I see it working as a video, it makes me cringe for myself. Because what I was then and what I am now – one of them has to be a fake! I just hope people realize that the old one was the fake. But I was completely into the idea of being screamed at – I was very young and I can't pretend my ego didn't need that. I was so into it that I didn't realize how hard it would be to come out the other side, because it has never been easy to make the transition from being screamed at to being listened to.

Andrew got more bad Press than me because he wanted that kind of publicity. When it all started the publicity he was getting was

At a party in Dad's restaurant to celebrate 'Go Go' becoming our first number one in Britain. Happy men indeed.

mainly that he was a bit of a lad, a lovable villain – Randy Andy. He didn't mind any of that, in fact he loved it. So he would actually go to places where he knew that he would be smashed out of his brains by the end of the evening and that they would get their pictures. He thought it was a laugh – it was only later that they tried to make him look like a real idiot. I was going out to places where the Press wouldn't be. They didn't particularly want to be at those places either because they didn't want Andrew and me to be the same. They wanted their readers to side with one or the other of us.

You can't win with the mass media because they don't have a healthy interest in anyone. You play the game, you get that initial excitement of being on the front page, and you pay for it later. And the whole Press explosion happened around the time of 'Go Go'. □

The first George Michael solo single, his own production of 'Careless Whisper', replaced 'Two Tribes' by Frankie Goes To Hollywood at the top of the British charts in July 1984. Before the record was released, the talk in the Press had been of a haircut that cost George £17,000. During the filming of the song's video in steaming Miami, the humidity had turned George's hair into a frizzy mess. He had ordered a halt to the shoot, flown in his sister Melanie to give his unruly locks a trim and then started all over again. The video consequently went over its £30,000 budget by £17,000, leaving George with rather a hefty bill for a cut and blow dry. Shirlie Holliman saw the completed video and said that, for the first time in her life, she felt a sexual attraction towards her old pair-dancing pal.

'Careless Whisper' changed a lot of minds about George Michael. Just as 'Go Go' had blanketed the planet for Wham! so 'Careless Whisper' took George around the world – the record went to number one in Britain, America (where it was billed as being by 'Wham! Featuring George Michael') Austria, Australia, Brazil, Holland, Hong Kong, Ireland, Iceland, Italy, Japan, Switzerland, Portugal, Venezuela and made the top five in another ten countries. During the few minutes that it took to play out the song's tale of temptation, infidelity and guilt, George grew up in the public's mind and laid the groundwork for his solo career.

□ *George:* In 1981 I was on my way to DJ at the Bel Air when I wrote 'Careless Whisper'. I have always written on buses, trains and in cars. These days it's planes – but for me writing has always been about boredom and movement. It always happens on journeys. With 'Careless Whisper' I remember *exactly* where it first came to me, where I came up with the sax line. I can remember very vaguely where I was when I wrote things after Wham! got off the ground – but with 'Careless Whisper' I remember exactly the time and place. I know it sounds really weird and a kind of romantic thing to say – but I remember exactly where it happened, where I was sitting on the bus, how I continued and everything. I remember I was handing the money over to the guy on the bus and I got this line, the sax line: der - *der* – der – der, der – *der* – der – der. Then he moved away and I continued writing it in my head. I wrote it totally in my head. I worked on it for about three months in my head.

February 1984, Miami. I was shooting the video for 'Careless Whisper', Andy came over with David Austin and we had a great laugh, probably because we were still unknown in the US.

CARELESS WHISPER VIDEO

£17,000 HAIRCUT

Andrew helped me in the finishing of it when we actually put it down on tape. I went to Andrew one day and said – I have this great melodic line but I don't know if it should be a sax or a vocal line. So he said – sing it to me. And he said – that really sounds like it goes with these chords I've got. And he had these four chords, the guitar lines.

He lived in this really awful, horrible flat with Shirlie Holliman. They tried to live there because I think that Shirlie wanted to get out of her house at the time and in the evenings we would sit there and try to write. And I remember we finished 'Careless Whisper' there. But really we did a lot more lyrical than musical collaborations.

Eventually, by the time we did our demo of 'Careless Whisper' and a couple of other songs, I had been given the sack from the Bel Air for always turning up late and for not playing the music that the guy in charge wanted me to. The place where I DJ'ed after that was a squash club – I was a restaurant DJ who had been relegated to a health club DJ. My DJ career had been all downhill.

But the very last night I ever worked as a DJ I played the demo of 'Careless Whisper'. I knew it didn't matter if I got into trouble because I had already given in my notice the week before. So right at the end of the night I played it and...the floor filled. They had never heard it before and...the floor filled. I remember thinking – that's a good sign. And I wondered what was going to happen to that song later on. □

A shot from the 'Careless Whisper' video. 'You're asking me to kiss a man with a wig on?'

CARELESS WHISPER VIDEO

SITTING ON A BUS...

Late in the summer Wham! adjourned to the south of France to record their second album at Château Minerval, the Provence home of jazz musician Jacques Louissier. As George painstakingly put together, *Make It Big* in the idyllic setting of Cézanne's countryside, the gap between the two halves of the band had rarely seemed greater.

□ *George:* It was unspoken, but I was very impressed with the realization that he had to do something to keep his personality up front because everyone was realizing the musical imbalance. I thought that it was a really good laugh, but the fact is that he was getting totally wrecked, he was so lazy and he just couldn't be bothered...Andrew would just turn up for a couple of days, do a few things, fall in the pool. That was the only time that I thought – oh, for God's sake, DO something. We did a special for *The Tube* and he arrived the night before so we could do this show down in the vineyards.

We woke up early the next morning because we had to start filming quite early, and Andrew was in the bath with all his clothes on. His mates Dave and Johnny were filling up the bath to wake him up and he was sitting there and I said – I can't believe it. You've only been here for eight hours, you only have one thing to do – wake up! Sober up! And I was slapping him around. And, sure enough, he was all right, he was actually very good in the interview, he was very witty and everything.

But for a while it really did do him some damage – not only did it get to the stage where he became a kind of laughing stock, but people were very jealous of him. He seemed to be getting too much for doing nothing. He was no longer seen as just a lad out having a good time. □

Make It Big was a number-one album on both sides of the Atlantic and confirmed George's position as a member of the new pop royalty, a status confirmed when one Sunday late in November he went to a studio in west London to help record Band Aid's 'Do They Know It's Christmas?', Bob Geldof's emotional – and effective – response to the famine that ravaged Ethiopia and the Sudan. The fact that Andrew did not join George and fellow pop toffs like Simon Le Bon, Sting and Boy George on that memorable Sunday was taken as increasing evidence of the lop-sided nature of the partnership.

□ *Andrew:* I got up rather late that day. I didn't even know that I was supposed to be going...By then it was clear to me that Wham! had achieved what George ultimately wanted it to. If he was really going to achieve his ambitions, then it would have to be on his own. As a concept, Wham! had become too restricting for him. □

'Make It Big' photo session, September 1984.

At Château Minerval in the South of France, recording 'Make It Big'.

Shirlie, early 1985, in a party mood and dress.

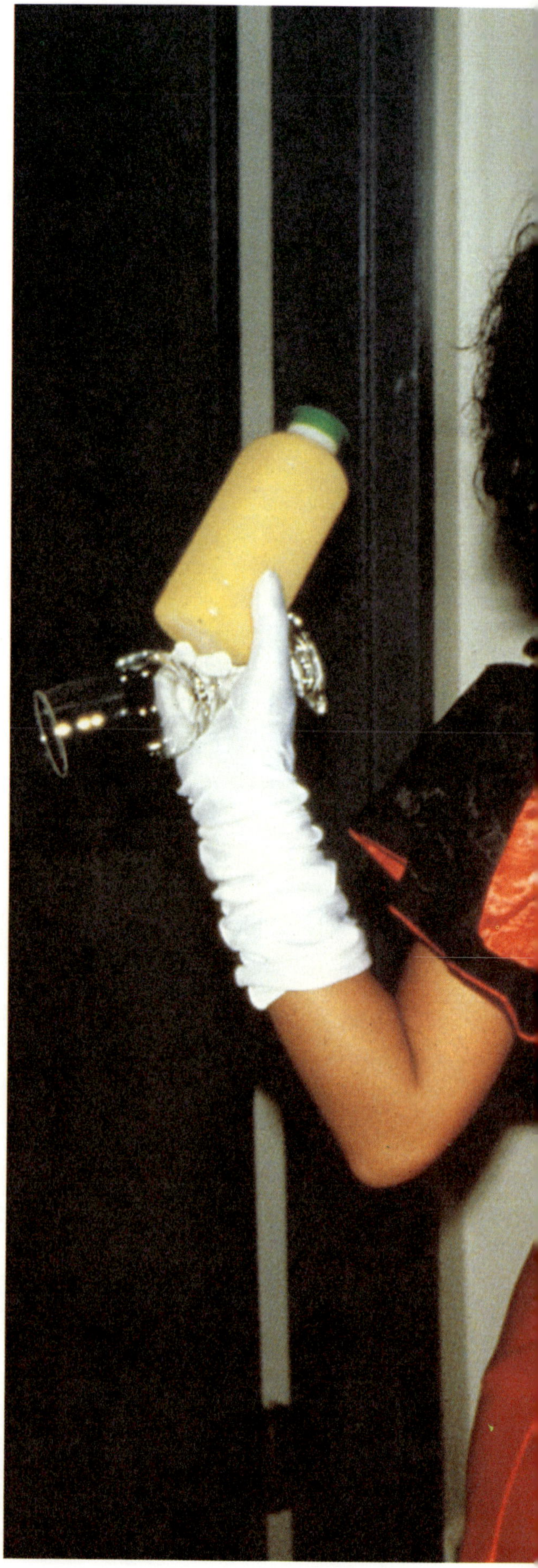

The early months of the new year maintained the giddy level of excitement that had become Wham!'s natural habitat. In February, two days after Valentine's Day, 'Careless Whisper', that sweet-sour ode to wasted love, went to number one in America. The following month, the British Academy of Songwriters, Composers and Authors voted George Michael the winner of the Ivor Novello Award for the Songwriter of the Year. George's old hero Elton John presented the award to him. He had already met Elton in Provence during the recording of 'Make It Big', but the emotion of the moment was overwhelming for the young songwriter and – for the first and last time – the control freak was moved to cry in public.

But mostly those early months of 1985 were spent enduring and savouring the treats and cruelties of life on the road as Wham!, following their winter trek around their homeland, went out and toured Japan, Australia and the United States.

□ *Shirlie:* The sad thing about touring was that George and Andrew stayed in different hotels from the rest of us. That was a big thing for me. I was always feeling, oh no, I'm in another hotel. It was done because of the fans. I felt the kick of it all, but I don't see what else they could have done. I didn't feel bitter. A lot of people around me at the time were saying: oh, they should treat you better than that, they're really dumping you. A lot of people were trying to stir it and when other people were saying things like that, it doesn't make you feel bitter towards them – George and Andrew – but it does make you feel more upset. People used to say to me, oh, they used to be friends with you but now those two are going off and leaving you behind. I never knew if they understood how I felt. There were these huge doors opening in their lives and they couldn't look back. □

On tour...

...with a hat.

□ *George:* Men are not used to being hunted. Initially, I thought it was absolutely wonderful. I really thought it was fantastic. And I abused the privilege a little bit maybe – although I wasn't getting anything out of a sexual situation that wasn't being returned. In fact, it got to the point where I realized that I was getting less out of it than they were and that starts to be a turn off...

Now I'm so aware of the fact that I'm a catch. The women are not the catch. *I am the catch.* It's not a very attractive feeling for me. Andrew doesn't mind at all. Andrew loves it!

But I'm not really into being the catch. □

□ *Simon Napier-Bell:* Number-one singles don't establish a name in America. But George didn't want to do the endless touring you had to do in America. George hated the Press, hated being photographed, didn't want to do radio interviews. Everything I knew you had to do to break through in America, he wasn't prepared to do. So I had to think of something else and right there at the beginning I thought – the first group to go to China.

It was a great publicity stunt but one that's easy enough when you think it up over dinner with a bottle of wine and quite different when you are confronted with the reality the next morning. I think I went to China thirteen times before I got it sorted out. I talked to the Government at the highest level. I was totally cynical about it – this was a publicity stunt to promote Wham! in America. As it began to take place one started to be swamped with accolades – this is the first cultural exchange since the Hong Kong settlement, this is opening China to the music industry. I was given an award in England by a Conservative minister for opening trade barriers.

It was real hype. We had to pay for everything – even for buses to bring the people in. The whole thing worked on total cynicism. Everyone who got a ticket was given two cassettes of all the Wham! songs, one for themselves and one for someone else. They could listen to the songs for a week and then, when they turned up for the concerts, they would be singing the songs. No one had ever heard of Wham! in China but the impression you got when you went to the concerts was that they were all very familiar with the group.

We were on every news bulletin – ABC, NBC, CBS – for a week, seven or eight times a day. At the end of the week everyone in America knew the name of Wham! That's what it was about – changing hit songs into a hit artist.

I had been to America the week before we went to China and when people said, what do you do?, I told them – they had never heard of Wham! But the week after I came back they knew immediately. That is what you have to do in America. In America you have to create a huge national story. Wham! did that by playing two dates in China.

I remember coming out of a hotel when we were in China in the middle of the tour and there was one of those big Chinese lions, a big stone lion, and someone had shoved a Coke bottle into the lion's mouth. George looked at it and said, 'That just about sums up what we're doing here.' □

With Andrew.

On stage in China.

Simon Napier-Bell and Jazz Summers called a Press conference to announce the release of two Wham! tapes in China. The first would be a compilation of material from the band's two LPs and the second would consist of five Wham! originals and five cover versions by Cheng Fang Yuen, the country's top female singer. Simon may have been thinking of Uncle Sam while he courted Uncle Mao, but he never lost sight of the fact that his research had revealed two-hundred million Chinese between the ages of eighteen and thirty-two. When it was revealed that Cheng Fang Yuen would get the basic rate of £15 for her work, George and Andrew were outraged and put her on a royalty.

After warming up with two gigs at Hong Kong's Coliseum Theatre, Wham! flew to Peking on 4 April where they were to play their first Chinese date at the ten-thousand-seater Workers Stadium on 7 April.

□ *Simon Napier-Bell:* I went back to China three weeks after the Wham! gig in Peking and the very same hall was being used for a trial of petty criminals who were being shot in front of an audience of ten thousand as each one was found guilty. Nothing had changed. □

Wham! played their Canton gig on 11 April to an enthusiastic crowd, the euphoria of the night unsullied by the fact that all the doors were about to be closed again.

The far side of the bamboo curtain. A fascinating but frustrating experience for me. Supposedly some kind of cultural milestone, in retrospect a sham.

By now Wham! were shockingly famous in England. One night in late spring George and this writer sat at the back of a very quiet oyster bar talking for a story in *The Face* and even though the table was at the back of the room – and George had his back to the window – cars were stopping outside to take a look at him. That night he talked about many things – the problems facing the contact lens wearer on a one-night-stand, the bitterness he felt towards the Chinese regime, his bond with Andrew, the privileged straitjacket of celebrity. He was open, intelligent, warm, ambitious, drunk. His driver waited for him outside the restaurant all night. George was twenty-one years old.

His confidence as a singer growing almost daily, George gave two high-profile solo performances within a couple of months. The first was at a Motown anniversary celebration at the Apollo in New York in May – the month that 'Everything She Wants' became Wham!'s third number one in the States – singing duets with two of the greatest singers of all time, Smokey Robinson and Stevie Wonder. Back in London in July, he sang Elton John's 'Don't Let the Sun Go Down On Me' at Live Aid. Andrew raised funds backstage and sang backing vocals, but to most people he was conspicuous by his absence.

First photo session with beard.

With beard and Andrew.

ON TOP OF THE WORLD

Live Aid photo session.

☐ *George:* I was aware that after Live Aid I was seen in some quarters as...a solo act. I was nervous as hell. It was the first time I had ever sung in front of an indifferent audience because every one I had sung in front of before had been mine – or ours.

More than anything, it showed that people wanted me – quite unfairly – to do stuff on my own so that they could admit to liking me. Everybody raved about my performance, which I honestly thought was very average. ☐

On stage at Live Aid with Bono, Paul McCartney, Freddie Mercury, David Bowie and Bob Geldof.

Wham!'s stadium tour of the States began in the last week of August, starting with two dates at the Illinois Music Theatre, then up to Toronto, down to LA (where they played Andrew's favourite Wham! gig at the Hollywood Park) and Oakland, across to Houston, on to Miami (where a girl in a bar pulled a gun on bass player Deon Estus) and Philadelphia the second choice on the East Coast after being unable to book New York's Shea Stadium, and winding up at the Detroit Pontiac Silverdome for the last date Wham! would ever play in America.

George dined with Brooke Shields at the Mayfair Regent Hotel in downtown Chicago, where Lake Michigan stretches off into the northern mists like America's third ocean. Up in Toronto he was offered millions if he would do a commercial for Pepsi Cola. Celebrity romance and lucrative endorsements – those Christmas bonuses of success – were calling him, but George was reluctant to heed their siren's song. As always, travel and boredom were inspiring him to write but the material he was coming out with seemed to stray beyond the borders of Wham!'s success. What he wanted was…out.

□ *Jazz Summers:* Worldwide the fans they had were crazy. I remember getting out of a car with George and these policemen were trying to hold them back. George had his hair pulled out and it was frightening. When they walk down a street and they are kids of eighteen, nineteen and a lot of girls scream at them – then they obviously think that's great. But take a look at their faces when they've been scratched and had their hair pulled out and their jackets are half torn off or their shoes – because fans just want a piece of them, anything, and that is truly frightening. George was shaken. Who wouldn't be? You're being mobbed.

During the second tour I took Yazz to Dublin one night and we all had dinner. And I remember George saying to the pair of us – I don't know if I can take this, I don't know if I can go through another thirty nights of people just screaming at me. □

ON TOP OF THE WORLD

STADIUM TOUR USA *AUGUST/SEPTEMBER '85*

Behind the scenes the pressure was beginning to build.

□ *George:* I can honestly say that I never lost my temper until I was twenty-two years old. And then for a period of about six or eight months before the end of Wham!, I really lost it. But I was blowing up in areas where normally I wouldn't. I was feeling *paparazzi* pressure at the time. One time I was with Shirlie coming out of Stringfellows and these two photographers jumped in front of us and – the flashes just seemed to set me off. I grabbed this guy and pushed him up against the wall – this is just so unlike me, being macho is not a normal occurrence – and started swearing at him, threatening to kill him. The other guy got a picture of me, just as I turned, with a really nasty expression on my face. The next day the papers ran a story about me attacking a fan and there was this thirty-five-year-old photographer with a Nikon strapped around his neck going – I will never buy his records again!

Another time I had a fight with David Austin outside Stringfellows at three in the morning. Absolutely awful! It was probably the most embarrassing thing I have ever done.

A huge insecurity is obviously the motivating force for most artists. And I understand that. But I feel that it's dangerous on a personal level to have a huge gap between what you are in your work and what you are in reality. The point at which I was most intimidated by my stage or public persona was when I was all teeth and silk shorts with Wham! I believed in it as a formula and I believed in it as a great way to entertain people but when I walked into a room full of people they had a totally wrong idea of what I was really about. □

□ *George:* I sat down at a table with Dick Leahy, Simon, Jazz and Andrew and said – I think this is the way it should go. Because I can't go on doing this, I can't write another album of material. This is no longer any good for me. All the time Wham! had been growing it had become more of a ball and chain. All the reservations I had about the character I was playing had become things that I really hated. I had to get away from the whole up-up-up thing because I felt so *down*. And I didn't know when I was going to feel good again. □

Late Wham! saw some of the group's most stirring work. 'I'm Your Man' matched the exuberance of 'Go Go' and 'Freedom', but had a muscular conviction about it that the earlier, poppier material had lacked. A beautiful, exhilarating single, it contained the ultimate Wham! line – '*Where we're going baby, ain't no such word as NO*,' – and went to number one in Britain at the end of November. The berserk, black and white video that promoted the song was shot at that most venerable of London rock clubs, the Marquee. Ironically, this was the venue where most bands started out and the place where Wham! was ending.

□ *Andrew:* But at least George and I managed to end it gracefully and with some taste. We did it our way. The music was actually very strong at the end. But one of the reasons it was getting good was because George knew it would soon all be over. He was about to do what he really wanted. □

'I'm Your Man', November 1985. Probably my favourite video, although 'Edge of Heaven' came pretty close. I don't now how I managed to look so bloody happy, I was depressed as hell. (By the way, the split had been finalized at this point.)

The Final 28 June 86

As was the Wham! custom before the important shows, the band played two warm-up gigs at the Brixton Academy on 23 and 24 June. The next day George celebrated his birthday. Three days later Wham! ended it all at Wembley Stadium on the hottest day of the year in front of seventy-two thousand people who had received tickets out of nearly one million applications. They could have played ten straight dates at Wembley and still had to turn people away. But The Final was a one-off.

□ *George:* That was a time in my life when I was drinking a lot and feeling generally run-down. It doesn't matter how good the day was – and the day was great – when you're that run down and depressed, it has to affect you. I don't think I rose above it even on the day of The Final. With a genuine depression it doesn't matter how good the highs are, there's always an undercurrent of depression that doesn't go away. Sometimes having a good time is not enough.

I really did enjoy the day and the concert very much, but looking at pictures of it now I can see that something was very wrong. Even with Andrew. I think we were both worried. He looks much more drawn than he did only a year before. He was doing a lot of drink and stuff as well and there were worries on his mind, I suppose. There was a lot happening to the pair of us.

But The Final itself was incredible – it was so important to me that it didn't register enough. There were two video tapes that were made of the monitorings on the screens and watching them is absolutely stunning. □

On stage at The Final.

The emotional programme notes hinted only obliquely at certain reservations about their success story (notably Andrew's 'We all wake up in the middle of our best dreams', and George's 'Of course, dreams aren't necessarily all they're cracked up to be') but at the end of the summer's day this was Wham!'s happy ending – they never got old, they never got greedy, they never came to hate each other's guts. The Final was where the dream died of natural causes. They were both twenty-three.

Stars, small and large, past and present, flitted across the stage. Gary Glitter and Nick Heyward primed a crowd that didn't need warming up, Elton John and Simon Le Bon joined Wham! on stage during their performance. But from the first song until the last, from the opening lines of 'Everything She Wants' – *'Some people work for a living, some people work for fun'* – to the closing lines of 'I'm Your Man' – *'If you're gonna do it, do it right'* – the true star was a bond as profound as the friendships of childhood. When it was over, George Michael – his hair dark and shorn short, a man all in black, dressed for violence or mourning – hugged Andrew Ridgeley, his perfect foil, his perfect friend. Then they went to the Hippodrome and got drunk.

With Elton in disguise.

On stage with Paul Young at Wembley Arena, 1986.

□ *George:* We were conscious that our relationship would be different from then on because we were no longer part of a band. I remember going up to Andrew at the party afterwards and giving him a big hug. And I remember looking at each other and…knowing really…it was sad. We knew that whatever happened, no matter how much we kept in touch, that from then on it was a totally different thing. And in some ways that was very sad, very moving.

No way could I have done it without Andrew. I can't think of anybody I have ever met in my life who would have been so perfect in allowing something, which started out as a very naive, joint ambition, to become what was still a huge double act but what was really… mine. I've never met anyone who would be strong or generous enough to let that happen. He contributed so much. It was one of those things that just makes you think it was all meant to happen. The luckiest thing that ever happened to me was meeting Andrew. He totally shaped my life. □

□ *Andrew:* I wish I could remember more about The Final. It wasn't even our best show – I don't suppose it could be, there were too many other considerations. It was difficult to enjoy the actual doing of the show, and difficult to call it all back…

The one I really remember best, the one that sums it up for me, was in Los Angeles. It was absolutely staggering because it was at a racecourse and there was this vast grandstand in front of us. There were about fifty-six thousand people there and they were all over the grandstand, all over the track. As it did at Wembley, our stage had these great big pincer arms. And it was a real hot night – just like Wembley.

We had a police motorcade to take us to the gig and George and I were cowering in the back because it was just so embarrassing, so ridiculous. The cops on their bikes at the front would zoom off and the two behind would zoom up alongside us and the ones in front would stop the traffic at the next crossroads…what a farce…It was all a bit special.

Now I don't get the chance to see George every day. I see him pretty often. But not as often as I would like. Not as often as I should. □

Backstage at The Final. It was a strange feeling. The proudest and saddest day.

THE FINAL

ANDREW

With Aretha in Detroit. It was a proud moment. Unfortunately, Ms Franklin wears glittery make-up, which stuck in my beard for two days.

The public reminder that George Michael was alive and kicking came out of Detroit. Recorded during the wind-up of Wham! but not released until early 1987, 'I Knew You Were Waiting (For Me)' – love those brackets – by Aretha Franklin and George Michael spectacularly bridged the gap between The Final and 'Faith'. The duet was instigated by the Aretha camp, who no doubt hoped that the winning combination of the Queen of Soul (and for once the hype is completely justified) and the Prince Regent of Pop would, as they say in the crossover-conscious record industry, broaden her base. This proved to be the case and 'I Knew You Were Waiting (For Me)' went to number one in Britain in February (keeping Shirlie Holliman and Pepsi De Marque's début single 'Heartache' at number two) and in the United States in April – Aretha's first number-one single for twenty years.

□ *George:* We recorded the song together and then did our libs separately. It was really easy to do; Narada Michael Walden is brilliant at getting a good atmosphere in the studio and making everybody feel at ease. I was nervous but, vocally, I was getting very confident at the time. I knew that Aretha would get the melody and then take it all over the place, which sounds great, but the thing also needed tying down. And I knew there was no point in trying to take her on in that style. I had heard the thing Annie Lennox did with her and she had tried to do it like Aretha. Now Annie Lennox is a great singer but *nobody* can emulate Aretha Franklin; it's stupid to try. I just tried to stay in character, keep it simple – it was very understated in comparison to what she did. □

'I Want Your Sex', June 1987.

The BBC effectively banned the song from its radio and television networks. MTV showed the video but only after much editing and many hot flushes. The song sneaked out into the world on the soundtrack of the Eddie Murphy film *Beverly Hills Cop II*, while back in London the George taskforce searched for outlets for the promo.

The controversy helped to consummate the image of George as a mature artist but the censorship certainly harmed the record's sales. 'I Want Your Sex' reached a paltry number three in England, the first George Michael single not to make it to number one since Band Aid kept 'Last Christmas' from the top.

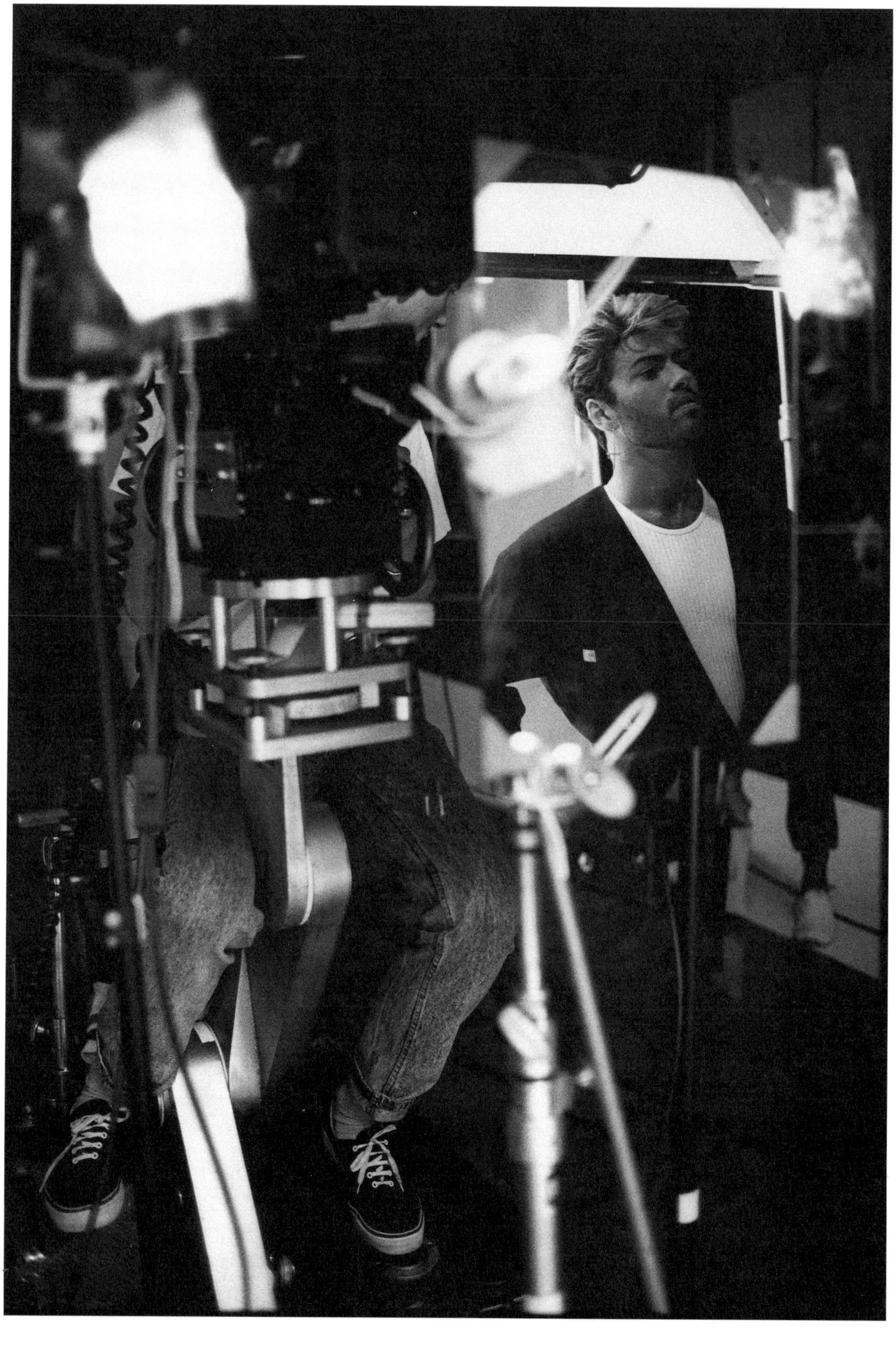

Filming the 'Sex' video. Make-up artist Lynn Easton, sweet though she is, spoils an intimate moment for the sake of a little powder.

Anyone who thought that strapping lad baring all in 'Sex' was me was sadly mistaken. Ever met a Greek without a hairy chest? And anyway, if I'd been doing it, I wouldn't have been able to watch it, would I?

☐ *George:* I still feel outraged by the reaction of a lot of people to that record. I expected it and in some ways it was good for the record, but I just thought it was so pathetic. American rap music and heavy metal are so aggressively sexual in a completely distasteful way – and I didn't think 'I Want Your Sex' was at all. ☐

Whispering sweet nothings.

After the year of coming apart – physically, mentally, professionally, this had been a season of coming together, a time of renewing faith, a time of benefiting from partnerships – the talk with Andrew, the record with Aretha, the link forged with Rob Kahane, the relationship with Kathy Jeungh, the project with his cousin Andros. In their own way, they had all given George a lot. And now he was strong and ready, about to go it alone, well and truly solo.

FAITH

THE MAN FROM FAITH

The title track of the 'Faith' album defined the look of the coming campaign and measured the difference between George in the late 1980s and the callow, clean-shaven youth who had appeared in the early Wham! promos. Once you went beyond the hoodlum chic – boots, jeans, biker jacket – the contrast was great. Early George had still been carrying the vestiges of puppy fat and, no matter how hard or often he scowled, he couldn't disguise the fact that he was deliriously happy to be part of the showbiz whirl. But the 'Faith' George was self-contained and self-assured, tanned and bearded, a man who wore his hormones on the outside, scowling, brooding, never smiling behind his hard-nut shades. This was nothing like the early George. It was also, of course, nothing like the real George.

□ *Dick Leahy:* When 'Faith' took off I heaved one of the biggest sighs of relief I have ever heaved in my life. Because with the break-up of Wham! I had a lot of people coming to me saying – you *have* to persuade George to do one more Wham! album. Lobbies go on. You can imagine. But I wouldn't do it. 'Faith' was the album he had to make. □

□ *George:* I remember my manager turning to someone in a meeting just before the whole 'Faith' thing began and saying, *he's going to be the biggest artist in the world after this album.* I remember saying to him – oh, calm down, for God's sake, really calm down. I put it down to American hyperbole, though he totally believed it. And these days when people say things like that, when they make all these claims on my behalf – even though I think it's wrong and I don't believe I've attained either the sales or the status to claim things like that – I still find it amazing that people are even *thinking* in those terms at this stage. □

'Faith' brings a new image.

'Faith' LP released November 1987.

FAITH

NEW MAN

□ *George:* 'Faith' was inspired by a couple of relationships that *didn't* happen. Very soon after the break-up of the group and before I started seeing Kathy, there were people who I played around with the idea of starting relationships with and eventually decided against them. Because I knew I was on the rebound and I wanted to be with someone for a different reason than that. I just decided that it wasn't worth it until there was someone that I felt reasonably comfortable with and that's what the song is about – just the idea of seeing someone and knowing that they're going for you, knowing that it's a possibility but, as much as it would be fun, it wouldn't be a very good idea.

I needed to believe that it was possible to get the things I wanted. At the time I wrote 'Faith' and the whole album I was with Kathy – so I did believe that I had pretty much got what I wanted. Now I'm not in that relationship with Kathy any more. But though the fact that it's over has made me feel bad in some ways, I'm still an optimist, I do actually have that faith. 'Faith' was about attitude, it was a whole attitude that I took on at the beginning of that part of my life. I meant it. I still do. □

A shot from the 'Faith' album session. I had seen Russell Young's work in Blitz and his use of high colour and contrast was similar to the video technique I had used for 'Sex', so I gave him a call.

FAITH

INSPIRATION

□ *George:* The 'Faith' image had a lot of restrained aggression in it. I don't think it's over-the-top aggression. It was the way I dressed at the time and very often still do – just a ripped pair of jeans, a leather jacket, those were the glasses I had been wearing, and the shoes too – and we just stylized it. I never considered it a particularly macho look but I tried to soften it just a bit by having a string of pearls on one of the shoulders of the leather jacket.

To me the album was about an affirmation of faith – because before that period of my life there had been a lack of it. As I said, coming out of the Wham! thing I felt as if some big joke had been played on me. I had led myself to believe I had everything – I'd dreamed of realizing certain aspirations and they had all happened but I still felt there was a big gap, a massive hole in my life that I was never going to be able to fill. That was the way I felt at the end of Wham! What 'Faith' meant – the album, the campaign, all of it – was that I had faith life was going to deliver, that I was going to get the things I wanted, that my life would bring me the things that are important to me. □

Well I guess it would be nice...if I could really play guitar.

FAITH

The first two solo singles, 'Careless Whisper' and 'A Different Corner', had moved George away from the gaga, go-go, finger-snapping image of vintage Wham! while the next two, 'I Want Your Sex' and 'Faith', clearly established that the solo Geroge Michael was not going to be restricted to singing showstopping, sob-in-the-heart ballads. Those later singles reflected George's divided soul – 'I Want Your Sex' had been black and funky while 'Faith' was as white and happy as an Elvis movie. 'Faith' – the album, the concept – was all about a renewal of belief, all about finding reasons for optimism and hope even after your heart had been kicked around the block. The five icons on the inner sleeve represented FAITH – MUSIC – MONEY – RELIGION – LOVE but 'Faith', the single, sounded as though it had lighter things on its mind. Released in October, it climbed to number two in England the month before the album release and saw out the year at number one in the States. Top of the *Billboard* Hot 100 was going to be a home from home for the coming year.

'Faith' the single released in October 1987.

□ *George:* I didn't expect the persona to do what it did in America. I expected to sell an awful lot of albums, but I genuinely believed that I wasn't vivid enough to take it beyond that. The actual video of 'Faith' is the strongest image of me off the album – the jacket, the jeans, the boots – and I didn't think that was far enough away from the way I really dressed to believe in it as some big visual statement. I wasn't comfortable with how strong that image became – because ultimately it begins to blur the reasons for your success.

But unless something happens in my life that really makes me change my mind, then I'm not going to be doing that any more, I'm not going to be putting an image out there any more. I was watching a tape of me two years ago and someone said – that could be you now. Hair's the same length, exactly the same type of clothes, all the rest. And that's a good reason for not wanting to do any more – I'm not capable of changing it again without it being false. □

□ *Andrew:* I never really understood why he wanted to portray that image – the brooding, macho guy of 'Faith'. That's not him. That's not how he is with his friends. As much as I think it's a great image and he looks fab, George away from the industry, away from the visual part of his music, is very different. □

Signing autographs.

□ *George:* When you look at 'The Final' album there are four or five different images in there and each one shows a different year and a different look. I was still a kid trying to work out which way I looked best. Did my hair look best short or long? Dark or blond? With or without a beard? It wasn't a David Bowie thing – I wasn't changing to keep people interested, I was just always dissatisfied, never confident. And I'm just not going to make that effort to go out looking different any more. □

FAITH

The year 1988 was consumed by touring – the 'Faith' tour began in Japan's Budokan Theatre in Tokyo on 19 February and would not end until the date at Pensacola, Florida, on the last day of October. In between were nearly a hundred and seventy shows and ten months of a lonely, peripatetic slog that was interrupted only for throat surgery. The tour, like George's career, had a westward drift – from Japan the circus moved down to Australia and then on to Europe before the long summer offensive on the United States.

□ *George:* There are times when I enjoy a sense of power but only on a small scale. There's a huge sense of power on a tour, which can be very uncomfortable. With the band and the crew, I'm their employer, I don't like being their boss, I don't like hearing people say things and wondering what they would *really* like to say. I don't like it if you make a decision on lighting or sound or on any one of a number of things and, even though I think I'm totally right, I *know* other people think I'm wrong. If I'm right or wrong all they can say is, OK.

But I definitely have an ability to terrify people without doing anything to warrant it. Part of it is the fact that you're the employer but mostly it's this barrier you're forced to keep up. I don't have that kind of relationship with Deon, my bass player, or Jake Duncan, my tour manager, because I've worked with both of them for a long time. □

On the move.

FAITH TOUR FEB/JUN 88

IT BEGAN IN JAPAN

Relaxing.

The 'Faith' tour was a very modern one. In the past, the wild men of rock and roll had found it necessary to surround themselves by all hues of groupies, dealers and even people to carry their 'stash' through customs. Instead of all these louche attendants, George Michael had a fitness trainer called Paul Corkhill on the road with him and together both men would work out for four hours every day.

Janet Jackson's anthem to autonomy, 'Control', started the show every night, but for the first five months of the tour it seemed to George that control over his destiny was receding fast. His larynx was proving maddeningly unreliable and, as the tour wound down through the Pacific basin in those early months, his throat was often paralysed with pain.

On stage.

□ *George:* I tried to counteract the absence of real people around by having friends fly out to the tour when they weren't working. Andros, David and Andrew all came out at various points, but what was alarming was that I couldn't really communicate with them. Andros and David came out together at one point and they were told by minders what they should and shouldn't do with me and how I had to be at this place at this certain time or they were blamed if I went out with them after a gig. □

□ *Andros:* I flew to Australia and as soon as I got there the bodyguards met me off the plane and said – you can't take George out, you can't do this, you can't do that. I was really offended. I thought, what do *they* know? They didn't grow up with this guy. But the security hated me. One night in LA it came to fists. This guy got me outside and started pushing me saying – don't take George out tonight. I said – if George wants to go out, he will. I walked into George's dressing room and said, George, tell this guy to back off. I was a bit drunk. George laid into him and the whole thing blew up. It got really heavy for a while. They hate to admit he thinks for himself. □

A press conference (my idea of a real-life nightmare) in Amsterdam at the start of the European tour.

FAITH

Andros and Co.

APAR

Wembley, June 1988.

The show reached London in early summer. George went to Wembley on the afternoon of Saturday 11 June to appear at the Nelson Mandela benefit.

The audience at Wembley for the Mandela concert was neither a partisan George Michael crowd nor the big-hearted happy family that had shown up for Live Aid. The funny man Harry Enfield correctly parodied the Mandela crowd's mindlessly hedonistic attitude with his line, 'Where is it? Where's my free Nelson Mandela?'

□ *George:* I've become much more cynical about benefits now. I had a horrible feeling about the people watching that Nelson Mandela show and what they would feel about African acts. Half of them were there to see Simple Minds and the other half were real thugs. I didn't like the whole thing. What I wanted to do was separate myself from any kind of self-promotion, I wanted to do something that would have nothing to do with anything that I was selling at the time. I didn't want to choose any material that had an overtly political message because I thought it would come across as really naff coming from me. So I thought the most political thing I could do was sing three soul records by artists who have influenced me. Stevie Wonder, Marvin Gaye, Gladys Knight. There was no other way I could have done it and still felt comfortable, and it was a great opportunity because you don't often get a chance to do those songs for a valid reason. Usually, people would think it's just self-indulgence. As it was, a lot of people criticized me and said they were bored and would have preferred to hear 'Father Figure' or 'One More Try' – very few people thought it was a good idea. □

□ *George:* In five months I went to eight doctors. They kept telling me it was just tour fatigue. When we got to London I said, look, I have to see a real specialist. I went to my own diagnostic doctor and asked him to recommend someone and he sent me to someone who gave me a much more thorough examination. He told me that I actually did have a very large cyst at the bottom of my throat and that I should have it operated on as soon as possible. That's when we took the break.

I was starting to be seen as temperamental or cracking up – and I knew that was nothing like me. Everyone was saying it was psychosomatic and I kept saying, look, if I didn't want to sing, I'd let you know. I had been through five months of my throat hurting like hell before the operation. At one point my mum said – I don't particularly want to come and see you any more because it hurts me to watch you sing. She knows me well enough to know, even from a great distance, when I'm in pain, when it's hurting.

After the operation we had a month off and I went to St Tropez. I wasn't supposed to talk at all but I was yabbering on. Then when we started up again in America we did forty-two dates, end to end, never missed a show. I knew it wasn't psychological. I knew I wanted to sing. □

Strike a pose, there's nothing to it...

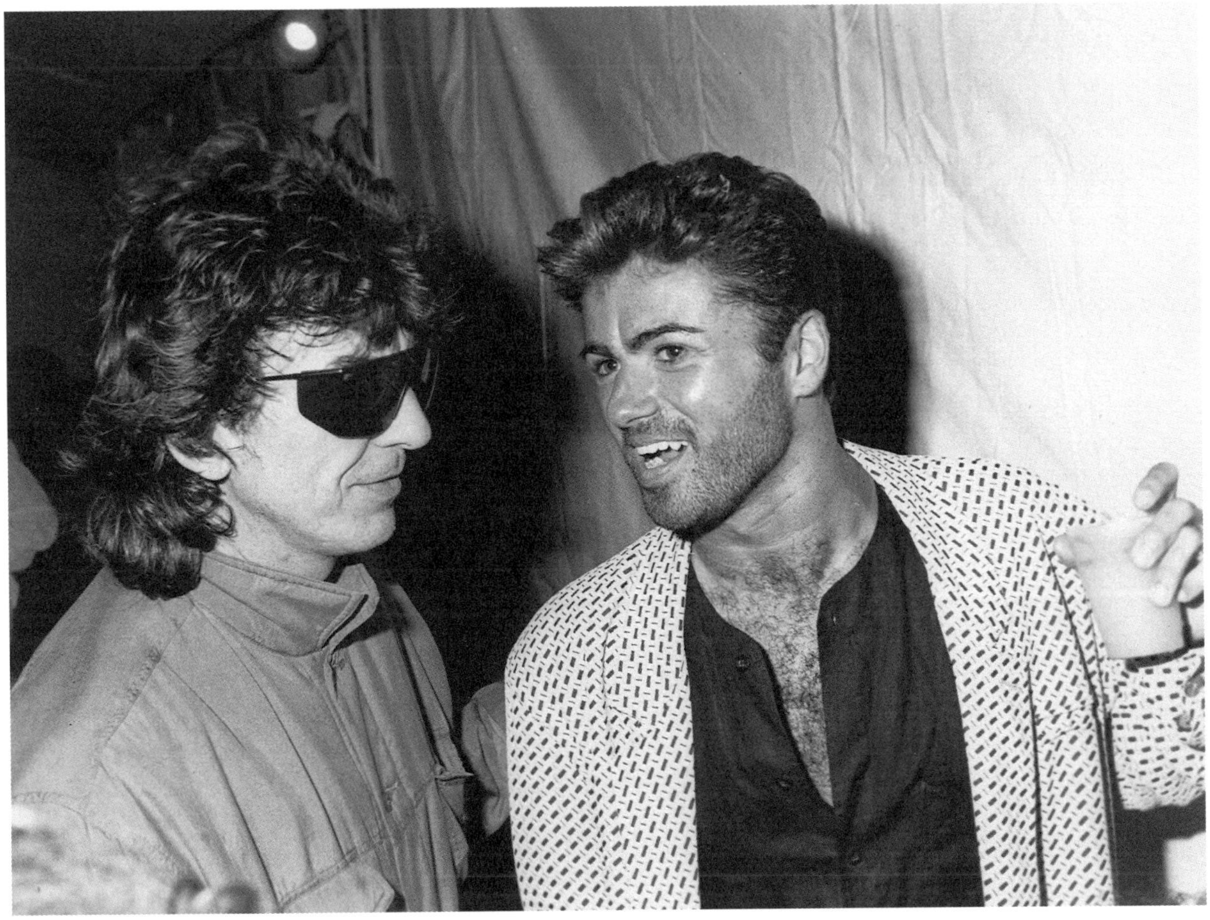

'Hey man, I mean, great music, but like, it always was a bit of a crap name for a band...' With George Harrison.

With Little Richard at the same tour party in LA.

□ *George:* To tell you the truth, I hate meeting celebrities. I've got a lot of time for Michael Jackson, he was very gracious to me, but on the whole I don't enjoy meeting celebrities. Not because of what they are like as individuals but because the basis of your common ground is so flimsy. What can you say? Oh, hello, so you're rich and famous too! Oh, so you're a celebrity too! What are you supposed to *talk* about? It's quite difficult. I tend to be the one who goes up to someone and says – look, I really admire what you do. And it's always true, I never say it to someone I don't feel that way about – and I have laid myself open to some nasty experiences that have made me shy away from talking to celebrities. If it's at all possible, I stay away from the situation. □

□ *George:* When you do a tour that long your life is on ice. It's a missing period for me, much more so than the down-time that preceded it. That's what I hate about the idea of touring, that's why I would never do it for that long again. It literally takes that time out of your life – and nothing happens. I mean, everything happens but nothing *really* does.

With musicians, session musicians, you never find a group of them who really believe in what they're doing. *Bands* belive in what they're doing. Session musicians maybe enjoy what they're doing, but it's not *theirs*. So, if you are soft, they'll take advantage, they won't get to rehearsals on time, and they will not always necessarily do their best. The only time they'll do their best is if there's some kind of barrier between you and them and they genuinely believe that, if they don't do their best, they're out. I never impressed that upon anyone. I didn't have to. □

Nearly ten months after the opening show in Tokyo, the final curtain came down on the 'Faith' tour in Pensacola, Florida, on 31 October. At the end of it all George had the year's biggest selling album in America, the Grammy for best album was in the bag and 'Faith' was the first LP to ever have six top-five US hits lifted from one album, nearly all of them number ones.

With the lovely Lynn Mabry, vocalist and dancer on the Faith tour. Some of our routines had to be, er, toned down, depending on where we were playing.

FAITH

□ *Dick Leahy:* In the past, George hasn't written enough songs. Elton John and David Bowie put out an album a year in the 1970s, sometimes two. You can't do that if you spend most of your time promoting – the sheer weight of making videos, doing interviews and touring makes it impossible. It's time-consuming, energy-sapping, and if George's basic love is songwriting and recording and arranging the stuff and getting it just right, then it's absolutely right that he should give himself the time to do that. There's no point in doing it if your frame of mind is not like that – but his frame of mind *is* like that and it's also the right thing to do. And that's when things work out.

He likes to spend time on the west coast of America, where he's bought a house. He likes the California sunshine. He's still got a lot of his old friends. He's very close with his family. And a lot of his life is very unreal. There was a lovely interview with him on American radio where the guy was talking to him about the pressures of fame. And George said, 'Look, I know I've said that it gets on your nerves but I must tell you there are some bloody good sides too. Every day you walk down the street and people *smile* at you. That's not bad, is it?' □

□ *George:* I want to step back from all the self-publicity and promotion and marketing to protect my ability, my gift as a songwriter. I think that if I've abused that gift it's been by not using it enough. I want to change that; I've realized I need to fight to protect that gift. But even more than that, I need to protect my life. It's not commonplace for people to get to the top of this profession when they're very young and then to live happily ever after. I realized that from an early point in my career and that's the most frightening thing of all. But I think if I step outside the promotion and the marketing of George Michael, doing all the videos and the big tours and interviews, then I have every chance of surviving as a successful musician and a balanced human being. I've achieved every other goal, I've done just about everything that I could. And that's my goal now. □

LISTEN WITHOUT PREJUDICE

□ *Andros Georgiou:* We go out for dinner every night. We don't know what else to do. We don't want to cook our Lean Cuisine at home. He's notorious for forgetting. He forgets everything. His car keys. His money. His credit cards. He forgets where he lives. Everything. Well, he remembered my birthday. He gave me a pack of Nike socks. Inside there was an £8,000 Cartier watch. A Panther – my dream.

If you're with George and his circle, you meet everyone. We went for dinner with Elton John a month ago and even now it's still hard for me. We grew up with Elton John, he was our hero. And Elton said, I've got my new album with me and I'd like to play you a few songs. We go to his Bentley outside the restaurant and listen to the new Elton John album on his tape deck. I said to George later – I can't believe it, we used to swap his albums. I would buy one, George would buy another, then we would tape them and swap. He was our ultimate hero and it's really difficult when you're sitting at a table with him. □

Andros

□ *Shirlie Holliman:* I think he loves people staring at him. Because he's such a quiet person, he's not like a loudmouth, there's no cockiness about him. But I think he likes people looking at him because we used to go to nightclubs and they used to clear the floor and we would just carry on dancing. That must have been a natural kind of high for him. He's a natural performer, a real exhibitionist.

I do think he's lucky. He's got people who care for him more than he knows. I care about him even if I don't see him. I always worry if he's happy or not. I always think – I hope he's really happy. He's earned it. When you see everything that's happened you think – I hope he's got that. □

Shirlie Holliman and me. 'George Michael is someone who has been made up,' she says. 'It's not someone I know.'

□ *George:* The things that get me down – like the lack of freedom or wanting to be in the right relationship or wanting an old relationship back – can only take up a certain amount of my energy these days, whereas they used to take up most of it. Obviously, the thing that's missing from my life is a stable relationship. But I don't wake up thinking I wish I was sharing my life with somebody. I've changed. Two or three years ago when I saw young guys in the park with their kids, I had this incredible sense of envy. It's gone.

I can't imagine living with someone. I would normally think, well, that's OK because everybody feels like that until they meet the right person, but I have a horrible feeling that part of my pleasure of living on my own is that my need for privacy is so much greater than most people's. It wouldn't matter if I met someone tomorrow and fell hopelessly in love with them and they felt the same, I would *still* always be George Michael to them. And even though they would get underneath that, part of them would still see me as George Michael and would always see me as George Michael.

And I can't take that. I feel a very great need to be away from George Michael most of the time. □

'Listen Without Prejudice, Volume One' was released in September 1990 and immediately went to the top of the charts on both sides of the Atlantic.

Those who thought that 'Listen Without Prejudice' was a defensive title got it wrong. When George Michael asked the world to listen without prejudice he was not talking about himself. He did not mean – please take me seriously. He did not mean – please forget you ever saw me wearing silk shorts and grinning like a loon with Wham! on *Top Of The Pops*.

What listen without prejudice meant to George Michael is that there are only two kinds of music. The two kinds of music are not black and white, AM and FM, pop and dance. The two kinds of music are good and bad. Listen without prejudice to all music was the author's message. Like we used to.

On first hearing, 'Listen Without Prejudice, Volume One' seemed to run the gamut of musical styles, just as 'Faith' had done before it.

There was the exuberant homage to Jazzie B's Soul II Soul, 'Soul Free', the joyous wake for George's late, unlamented teen stardom, 'Freedom 90', the mournful grandeur of 'Praying For Time' (it's tough at the top, was the song's thought for the day – and even tougher at the bottom).

George sang of beggars in the street, of love lost or misplaced, of the golden cage of celebrity. But despite all its upbeat moments, ultimately the overall mood of 'Listen Without Prejudice, Volume One' was a kind of controlled sadness, a wistful reflection. "You can't always get what you want," he sang on the sour-sweet 'Waiting for the Day', briefly quoting the Rolling Stones. "You can't always get what you want."

'Mother's Pride', released on the eve of the Gulf War, was an old-fashioned protest song bemoaning the young lives that are invariably ruined by war (ironically – or perhaps not – it became a great favourite with the troops out in the Middle East).

Mostly, though, George sang about his favourite subject – himself. 'Something To Save', 'Waiting For The Day' and 'Cowboys And Angels' were lush, introspective exercises in melancholy, while 'Heal The Pain' was the story of a modern love – damaged boy meets damaged girl and tells her it is not too late to try again.

Beautiful songs and bruised hearts – often 'Listen Without Prejudice Volume One' seemed like pages torn from a very private diary. Superbly crafted, lovingly expressed, many of the songs still sounded like confessions from a man who had been kicked around the block by love, who was still feeling the pressure of public misconceptions and who was still wrestling with his place in the world. 'No one can keep me from my destiny,' he sang on Stevie Wonder's 'They Won't Go When I Go', the only song on the album that he didn't write himself.

It was a great album, rapturously received by the media, the public and the record industry alike. 'Listen Without Prejudice Volume One' sold six million copies worldwide (it went triple platinum in the United Kingdom), received rave reviews even from hardened rock hacks and earned George another armful of awards, of which Sexiest Male Artist in *Rolling Stone* magazine's Reader's Poll was possibly the least, while Best Album at the Tenth Annual Brit Awards was probably the most meaningful.

The album achieved all this without the aid of promotion. George had been true to his word. The world tours, the endless interviews, the infinite videos to push singles that makes the music business go round – and that had done so much to make 'Faith' a huge success – all this was rejected as George concentrated all his energies on making more music.

With Elton.

There was no video to promote 'Praying For Time', which stopped rising higher than number six in the British charts, and only a few selected interviews – and these only to explain why he wasn't going to be doing any more interviews.

"I don't want to sell myself anymore," George told Adrian Deevoy in *Q* magazine. "And not just that, I really don't want to be visible anymore. I still really love making music and I still really want people to like my music. But I want them to like it for what it is. I'm not overly concerned about selling millions of records."

So serious was George about retiring from the harsh, empty lights of publicity that there was not even a picture of that familiar hairy face on the cover of 'Listen Without Prejudice, Volume One'. Instead the record featured a black and white photograph by Arthur Felig, alias Weegee, taken at Coney Island on 28 July 1940 at 4 o'clock in the afternoon.

Weegee specialized in the sleazy underbelly of New York City - he was possibly the greatest crime photographer of all time and did a nice line in dead gangsters, the casualties of domestic violence and weeping relatives. But Weegee, in his lighter moments, also took photographs of New Yorkers at play and it was one of these shots that George chose for his album's cover. But for all its sun-soaked fun and frolics, Weegee's portrait of the teeming crowds at Coney Island evoked feelings of claustrophobia as well as freedom. As that sea of individuals - trapped by their fellow man even when they are at play - turn grinning, waving and gesturing to the camera, it is possible to glimpse the view of one of the most famous men on the planet, a man whose every exit from a restaurant or change of haircut was considered to be of public interest. One look at that photograph and you knew a little of what it was like to be George Michael.

George's decision to withdraw from promotion drew flak from unusual quarters. Frank Sinatra was one of his most outspoken critics, claiming that George should be more grateful for his blessings. In a wonderfully pompous letter to the *Los Angeles Times*, George's new 'agony uncle' urged him to "Dust off those gossamer wings and fly, Talent must not be wasted. Come on, George. Loosen up. Swing, man." Translated, this saw Frankie trotting out the usual line – George Michael no longer wants to be famous, George Michael is not grateful for all he has, George Michael is a spoilt brat.

In fact George Michael was counting his blessings on a regular basis. He had opted out of the promotional circus so that he could concentrate on doing what he does best – making music. George was also reluctant to take advice from a man who did not walk down the street without a retinue of hired 'beef'. George Michael walks down the street alone. He likes it that way.

One of George's rare outings into the limelight at this time was when he was the subject of a *South Bank Show*, London Weekend Television's prestigious arts flagship. George was naturally flattered to be keeping company with Charles Dickens and Laurence Olivier rather than Prince and Kylie, though the programme was stuffier and more stilted than any young musician deserved.

Though there had been no video to sell the first two singles from the album (which may have hurt sales in Britain but didn't stop 'Praying For Time' reaching number one in the USA), the third single, 'Freedom 90' was supported by a promo. It was a bit of a non-promo – once again George Michael's face was nowhere to be seen. Had he been horribly disfigured in a car crash? No, but his loathing of advertisements for himself was hardening.

The video for 'Freedom 90', George pointed out, featured much nicer faces than his own. It was hard to argue with him. Super-models, Linda Evangelista, Tatjana Patitz, Christy Turlington, Cindy Crawford and – most super of all – Naomi Campbell, were hired for rather enormous sums of money to slink about miming the words to 'Freedom 90' – 'I was every little schoolgirl's pride and joy and I guess it was enough for me' – while symbols of stardom (the Faith-era biker jacket, juke-box and guitar) were ritualistically burned, blown up and generally destroyed. No pop star had ever taken such sadistic delight in trashing his stage clothes.

But, despite the tabloid sneers that George was turning into Greta Garbo with a beard, the man was still in love with writing, singing and performing. Shy and retiring he might be but he was still a trouper and a series of George Michael concerts – the first since 1988 – were scheduled for early in 1991.

'This is my first appearance in the Nineties,' George told the doting crowd in the NEC, Birmingham, on 15 January, the first night of the Cover To Cover tour, 'and it's a different kind of show.'

No kidding! If Madonna came on and chose to replace all the songs that made her famous with a selection of tunes that she had loved as a girl, then she would no doubt be booed off stage. If Prince decided that rather than play all his big hits, he would like to perform a number of Chicory Tip and Sailor songs that he had always been quite partial to, then ripe tomatoes would rain down from the auditorium.

But – sporting his new, close-cropped 'Terminator' haircut – George Michael marked his first British concert in almost three years with a set that was comprised mostly of cover versions of other people's songs – and he got away with it. More than that, it was a triumph.

Partly this was down to the quality of material he sang. There were barnstorming Tamla Motown classics like 'Papa Was A Rolling Stone', 'Baby Don't Change Your Mind' and 'Superstition' (George always loves singing Stevie Wonder). And there were songs of infinite sadness like the Eagles' 'Desperado', Boy George's 'Victims' and Elton John's 'Don't Let The Sun Go Down On Me'.

He sang the work of his heroes, influences and peers. He was taking a chance and he knew it. Towards the end of the evening, wreathed in a pearly smile (what you notice first about his bathroom are all the toothbrushes), George admitted how nervous he had been and rewarded the crowd's support with some gems from his own back catalogue - 'Freedom', 'Everything She Wants' and 'Careless Whisper'. The house liked this stuff even more.

Why did he do it? Why did the only British star who is in the same league as Madonna, Springsteen, Prince and Jackson, risk a disastrous comeback gig by not playing all the old hits or, even more to the point, material from his new album? Because he really did mean all that stuff about withdrawing from relentlessly selling himself. Because, after ten years at the top, he felt suffocated by the promotional demands of the record industry. This self-made multi-millionaire had gone into the music business for the music, not the business. He was in a position where he could refuse to play all the asinine old games. But most of all, perhaps, he did it because it was fun.

Stripped of all ambitions to plug George's latest "product", the Cover To Cover tour was a curiously joyous experience for audience and artist alike. George was having a good time and the admirably tolerant crowds, who never once called out for "Bad Boys", caught the mood.

The Cover To Cover tour headed to Brazil for the Rock in Rio festival at the Maracana football stadium, where Andrew Ridgeley joined George on stage for a brief Wham! reunion, and then came back for more English dates, culminating in stunning sold-out dates at Wembley Arena, with the exterior of the stadium decked out in a monumental blow-up of the Weegee photograph that adorned 'Listen Without Prejudice, Volume One'. Everyone who entered Wembley Arena for the Cover To Cover shows was given a four track cassette – a present from the man – which featured George's versions of Stevie Wonder's 'I Believe (When I Fall In Love It Will Be Forever)' and Gladys Knight's 'If You Were My Woman' plus the 'Back To Reality' mix of his own 'Freedom' and a new song called 'Fantasy'.

The tape served as both George's thank-you note to the fans and a taster of what was originally planned to be 'Listen Without Prejudice, Volume Two'. The album was at first scheduled to feature one live side of cover versions recorded during the tour and one studio side of George Michael originals. George later changed his mind and announced that the next album would feature just his own songs. The material recorded on the tour will possibly be released at some later date.

After that last night of the tour there was a star-spangled party in a Covent Garden nightclub where the famous faces did not include a certain famous English international footballer who was turned away at the door (either because he wasn't on the guest list or because the doorman was an Arsenal supporter).

George spent the summer months of 1991 mixing in Los Angeles. Autumn saw more work in the studio on the third George Michael solo album and the unveiling of the Cover To Cover tour in the United States.

For George himself, the highlights of the Cover To Cover tour were his versions of the Temptations' 'Papa Was A Rolling Stone', Stevie Wonder's 'I Believe', the show-stopping 'Calling You' (the theme from *Baghdad Cafe*) and Elton John's 'Don't Let The Sun Go Down On Me'. For 'Don't Let The Sun Go Down On Me' – which George first sang at Live Aid, his global debut as a solo singer – he was joined on stage at Wembley by Elton John himself.

The duet with Elton was released as a single in November 1991 and, after the tragic death of Freddie Mercury a few weeks later, it was announced that all royalties from the record would be donated to the AIDS organization the Terence Higgins Trust. 'Don't Let The Sun Go Down On Me' went to number one in the UK on 1 December.

As he said on stage at Birmingham on the first night - the Cover To Cover tour was a different kind of show. To those in the audience younger than George Michael - he was 29 years old on 25 June, 1992 - many of those classic songs were completely new.

Among his own new music that he worked on during the summer of 1991, George expanded on the canon of dance music that he had been creating since the early days. To many George Michael fans, this soulful, funky, black-influenced music is what he does best of all. Anyone who liked Wham!'s 'Everything She Wants' or 'I Want Your Sex' on 'Faith' or 'Soul Free' on 'Listen Without Prejudice, Volume One' could see their sweet, dark shadows on the music he was creating in the studios on Los Angeles and London.

If this new music was different from the dance music he had created in the past then it was because now George Michael was no longer mining the rich seam of traditional R & B. The inspiration was not what he had once heard on the radio, but what he was hearing in the clubs.

This music - songs like 'Fantasy', 'Happy', and 'Crazyman Dance' - relied more on rhythm and feel than the dance music George has recorded in the past. But unlike too much of contemporary dance music it never completely lost sight of the melody. It was still recognizably George Michael and among the greatest music that he had ever recorded. However, none of these new songs had their place assured on the next album. That would be decided much later.

As George worked on his next release, his tour and his tan out on the West Coast, back home in London, as always, the George Michael rumours were sprouting faster than facial hair on a Mediterranean beach bum. George lunched with Alek Keshishian (the hot young director of *In Bed With Madonna*) which soon had the press assuming that we were about to be treated to an *In Bed With George Michael* cinema-verite extravaganza. Unfortunately this was not going to happen. Although George Michael has great respect for Madonna, they are very different personalities. George is just not the type to allow a camera crew into his bidet.

By stepping back from everything that was not directly related to making music he was on target to do what his heroes like Elton John and David Bowie did in the 1970s - namely, make a record every year or so. And make it good. It's what he is here for.

Frank Sinatra should be applauding. That George Michael - he did it his way.

Listen.